The BOGO Colts And Friends

A Creative Coloring and Doodle
Book for Enthusiastic Artists
of All Ages

Within the pages of this coloring book, you will find a number of beautiful and whimsical designs to enjoy. This book is design to inspire your own creativity as I have included varying levels of complexity in the details and I have also included blank horses in the back for you to print and doodle your own patterns as many times as you like. You will find that some of the backgrounds aren't as intricate as they could be– it is my hope that you use your imagination and add your own finishing details before you color. A unique feature of this book is that all of the images are based on photographs of real horses that I have had the pleasure of owning or breeding; their names are on each of the facing pages along with the original photograph. So, grab a pencil, a pen, and the coloring tool of your choice and get started! Please feel free to share your completed pictures with me at bogocolts@gmail.com.

~ Jennifer Wilson

This book is dedicated to my family who has been so patient with me this past year while I wrote a novel and created three different coloring books. I can't thank them all enough for their patience and support in this new endeavor of mine.

The Sweet Rose and
Maghnus Z+//

~ Maghnus Z+// is proudly owned by Jay and Maddy Winer

PA Arbiter

~ PA Arbiter is proudly owned by Fallon Wortham

Majus ZF

~ Majus ZF, aka Luke, is one of the BOGO Colts, the
beautiful twin Arabians

Majician ZF

~ Majician ZF, aka Bo, is the twin brother to Majus ZF and
is the other BOGO Colt

Gasazi

~ Gasazi is proudly owned by Jim and Lori Hudson

The Sweet Rose and
Alia Bey Morafi

Eliron Haman

~ Eliron Haman is proudly owned by Angela Norton

Maghnus Z+//

~ Maghnus Z+// is proudly owned by Jay and Maddy Winer

PA A-Magic Moment, dam of the BOGO Colts

~ PA A-Magic Moment is proudly owned by Lori Watson

Alia Bey Morafi

The Sweet Rose

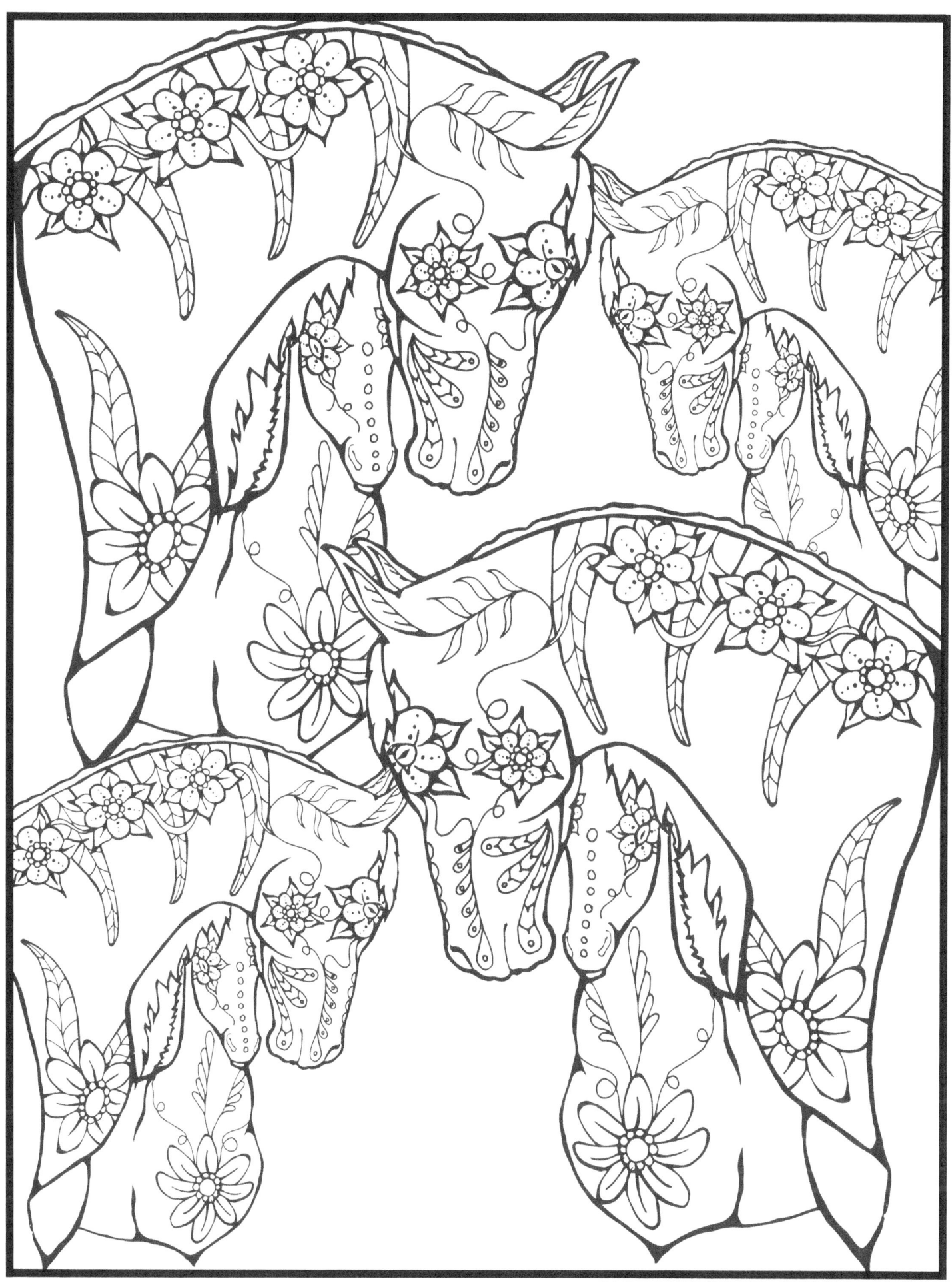

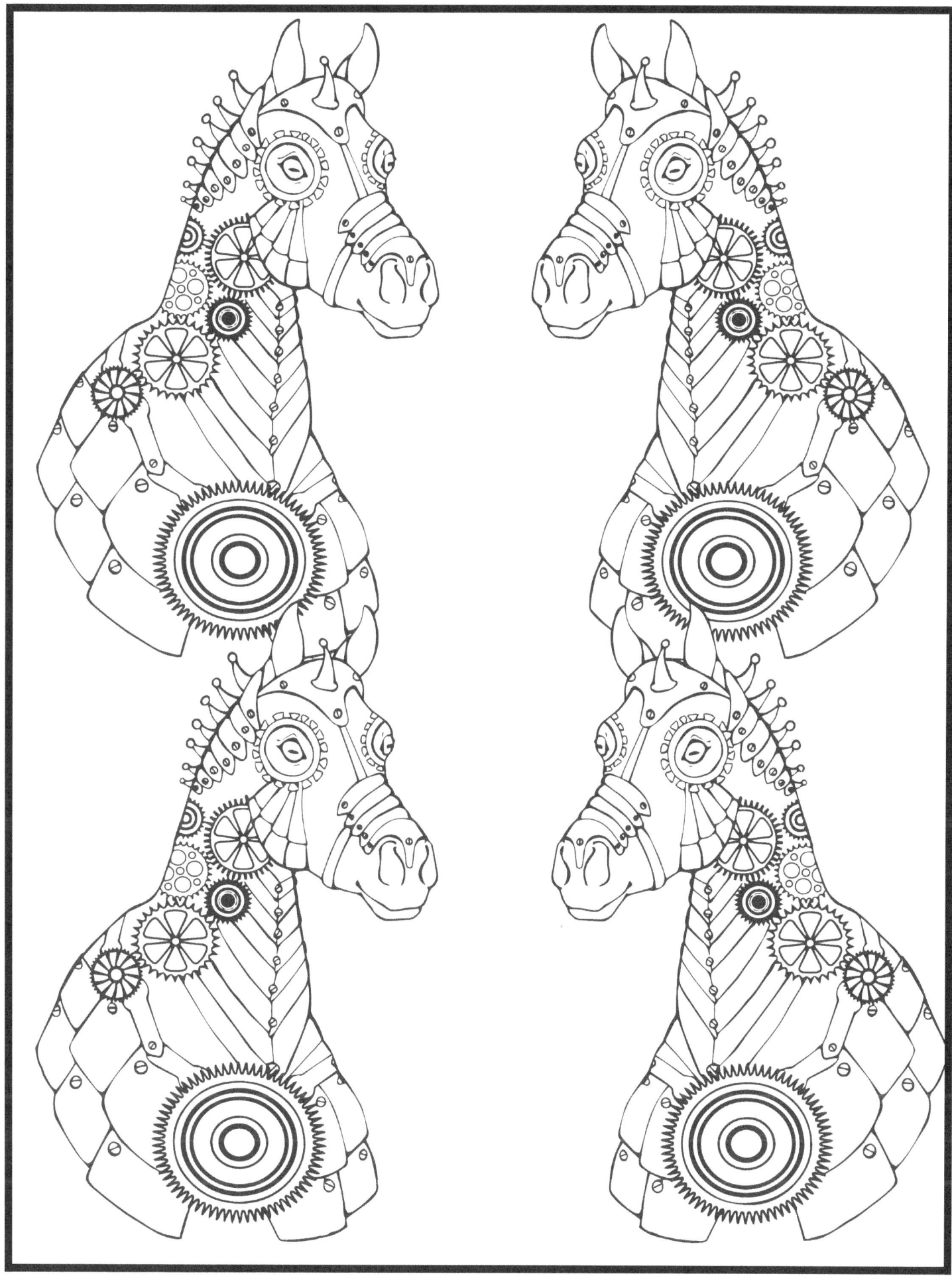

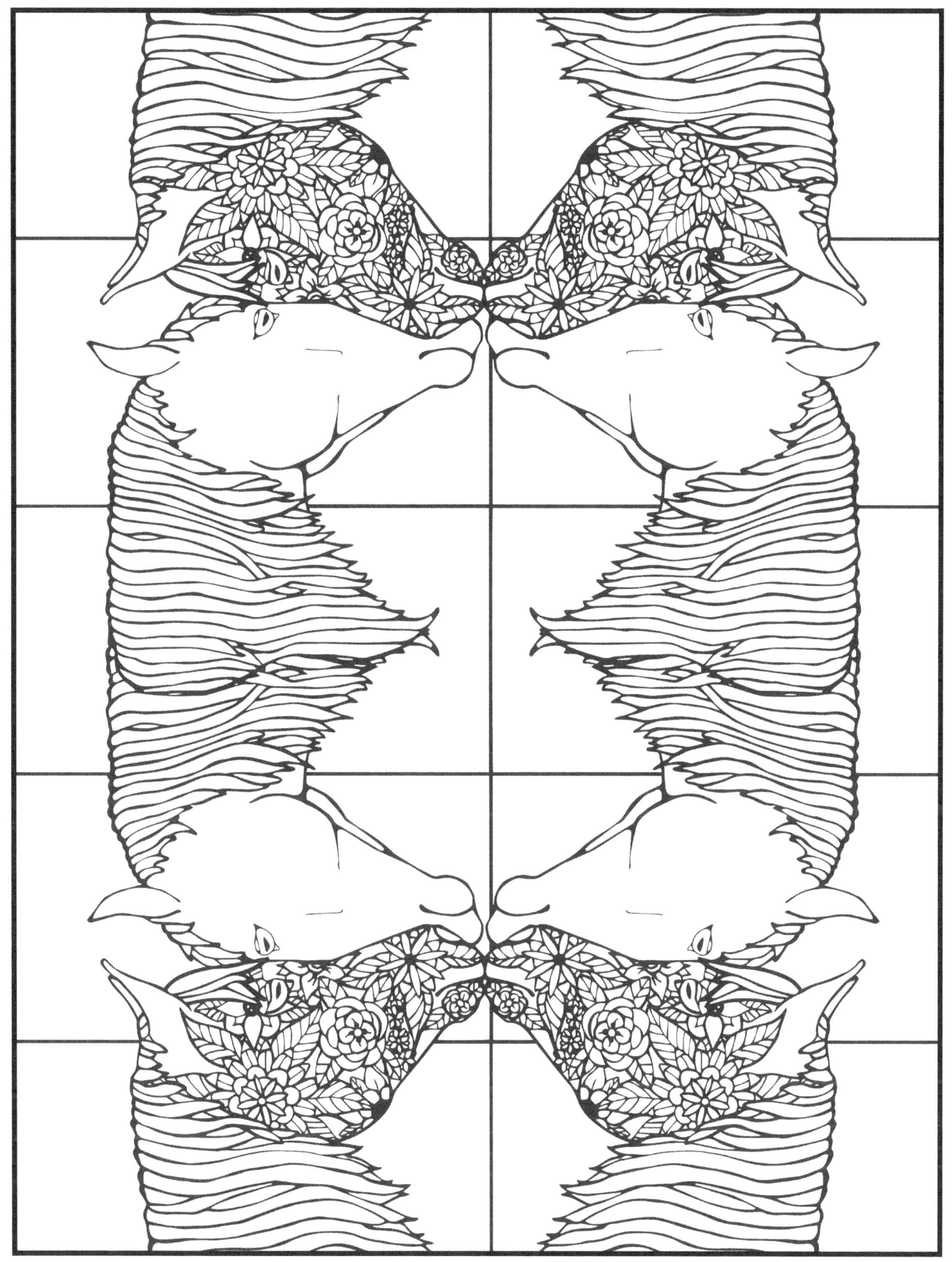

.

The following section includes the blank sketches I made of the horses before applying the creative styles. You have permission to copy and print the following pages as many times as you wish for your own personal enjoyment. There is also a page for bookmarks that you can print on heavy card-stock, add background designs, color, and enjoy! Let the creativity flow!

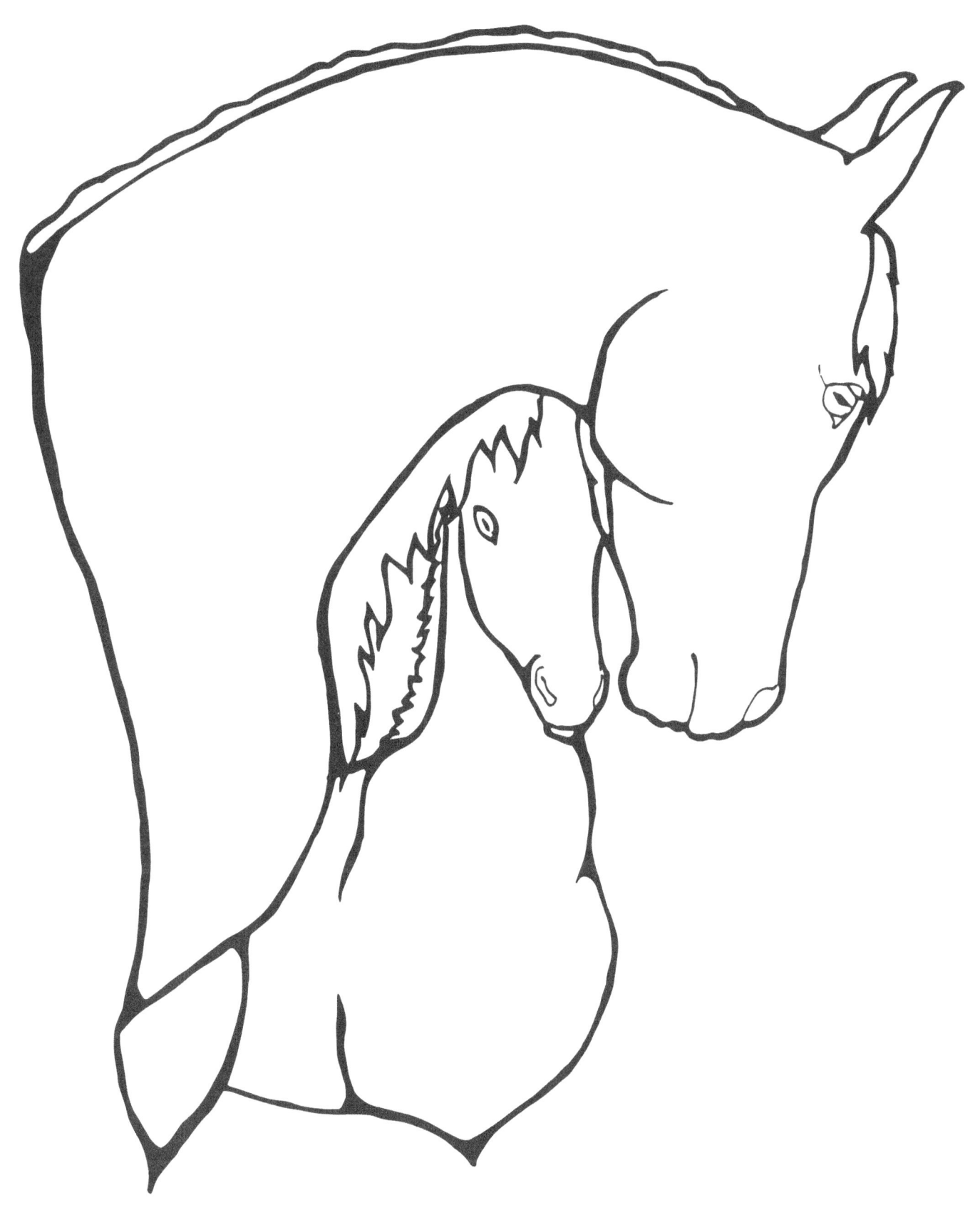

This image may be copied and printed for personal use

This image may be copied and printed for personal use

This image may be copied and printed for personal use

This image may be copied and printed for personal use

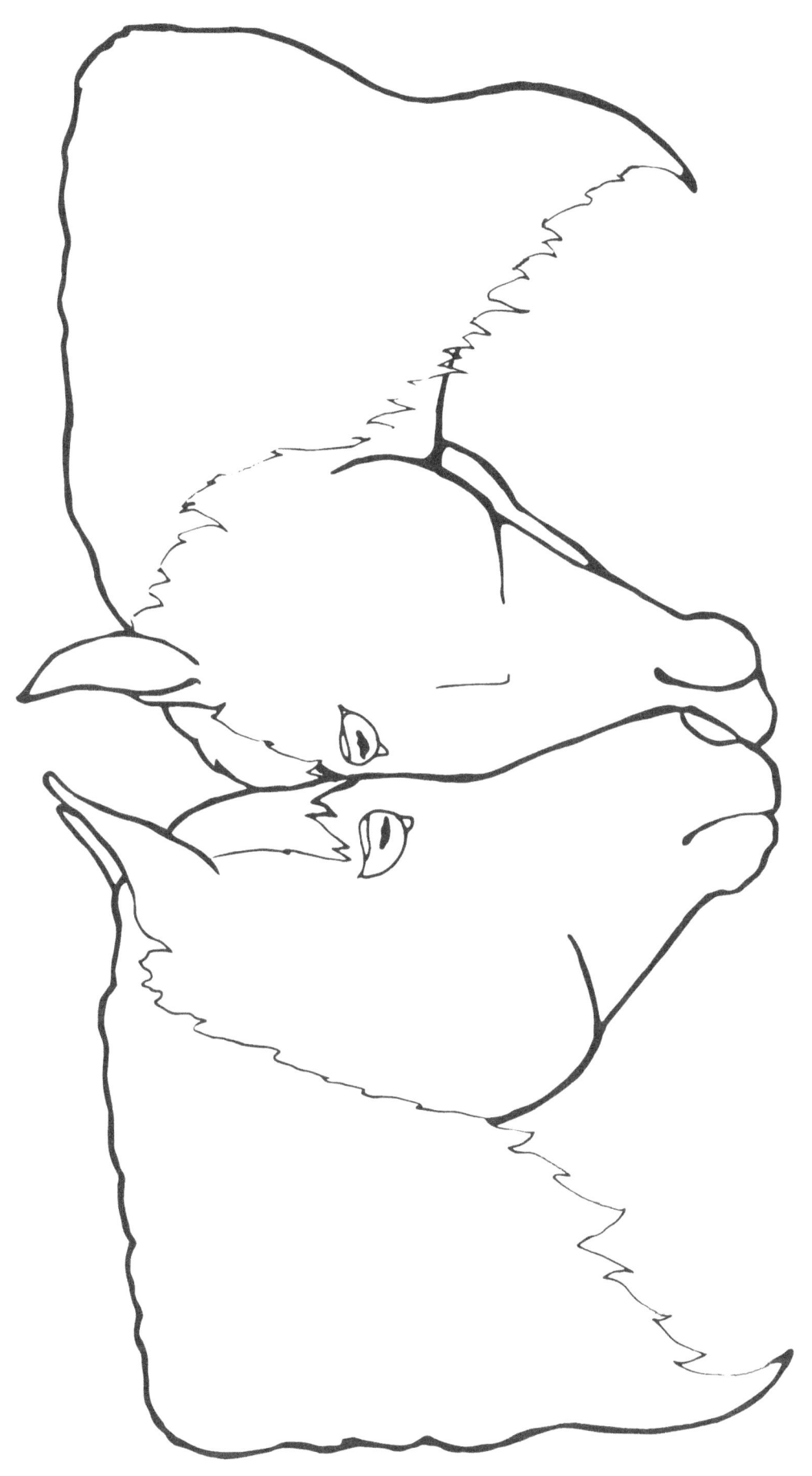

This image may be copied and printed for personal use

This image may be copied and printed for personal use

This image may be copied and printed for personal use

This image may be copied and printed for personal use

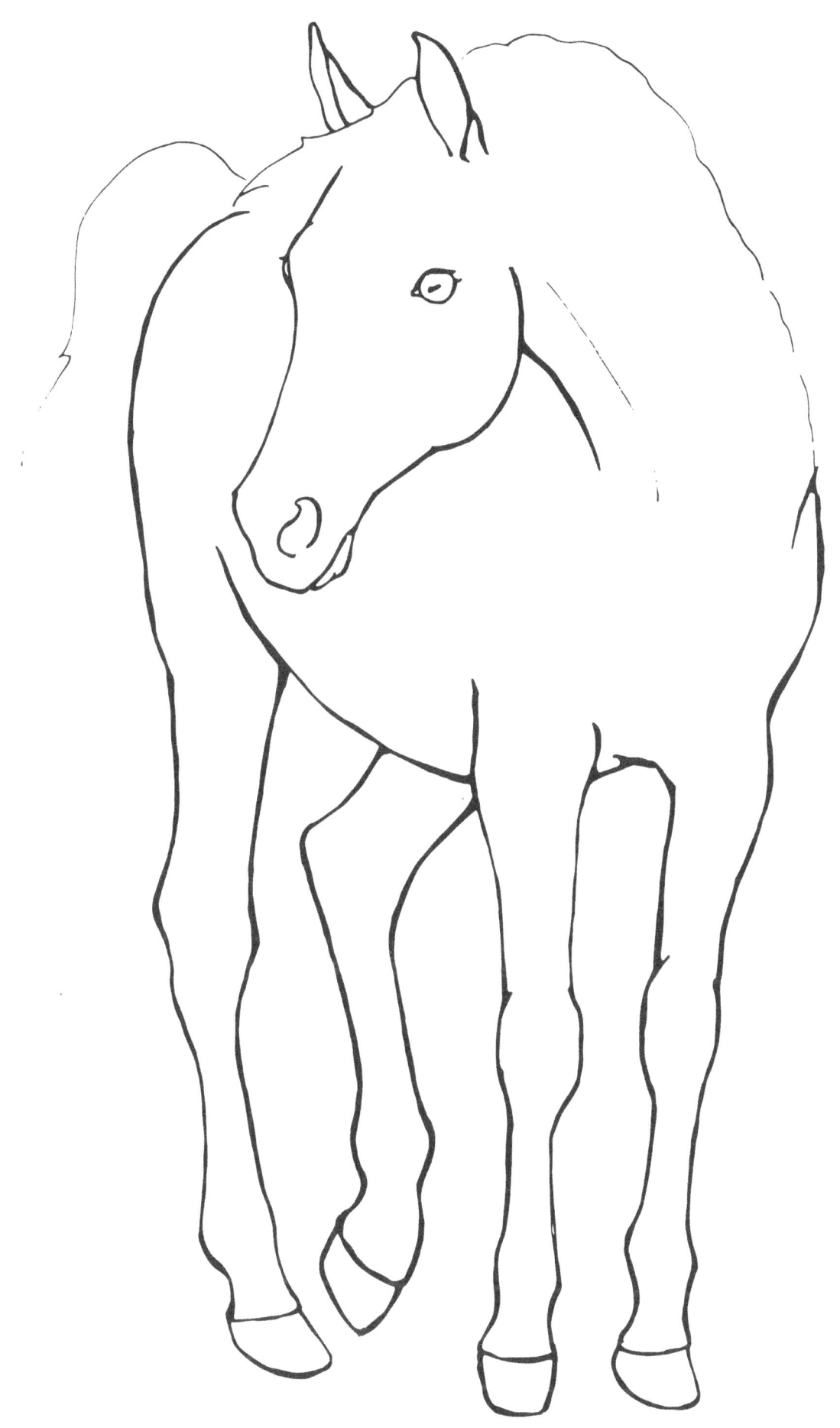

This image may be copied and printed for personal use

This image may be copied and printed for personal use

A Heart Full Of Hope

The True Story of the BOGO Colts

By: Jennifer Wilson

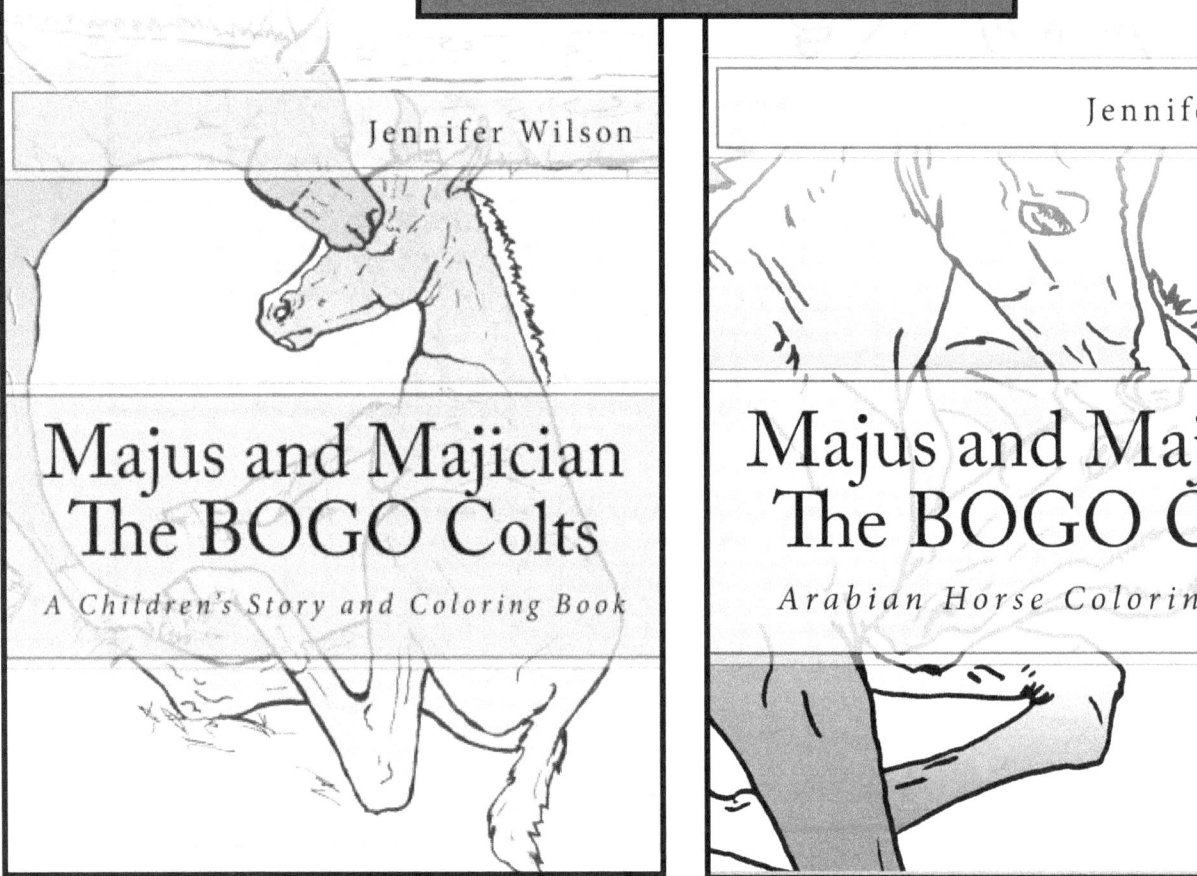

Jennifer Wilson

Majus and Majician
The BOGO Colts

A Children's Story and Coloring Book

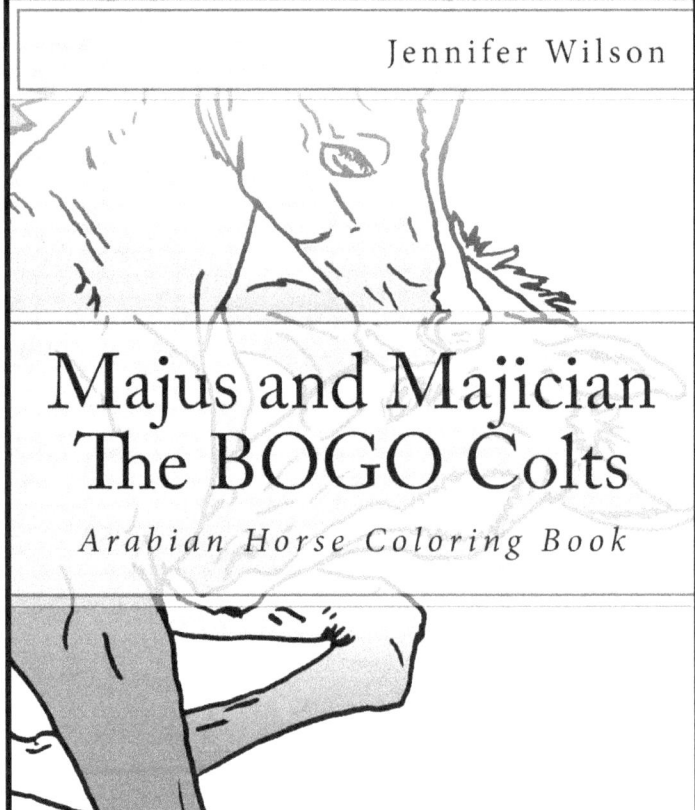

Jennifer Wilson

Majus and Majician
The BOGO Colts

Arabian Horse Coloring Book

Thank you so much for purchasing our creative coloring and doodle book. A portion of all of our proceeds are donated throughout the year to a variety of equine-related organizations.

You can read the full story of the BOGO Colts in their novel, *A Heart Full of Hope*, written by me, Jennifer Wilson. Majus and Majician are two amazing colts who have changed our lives. We hope you find their story incredible as well and that they inspire you to live your dreams.

Both their novel and their annual coloring books are available at online retailers such as amazon.com. They also have a children's coloring story book that is a must have.

You can keep track of news and shop for exclusive BOGO Colts merchandise at their website, http://www.bogocoltsbooks.com .

Order their annual calendar, our annual amazing Arabians calendar or their baby calendar at http://www.lulu.com/spotlight/majusmajician.

The BOGO Colts are going to star in an upcoming middle grades fictional series! Be sure to get exclusive sneak peeks, enter for free give aways, and follow all of the exciting release news at their Facebook page: http://www.facebook.com/bogocoltsbook

Thank you for following Majus and Majician, the BOGO Colts!

~Never stop believing in your dreams~

www.ingramcontent.com/pod-product-compliance
Lightning Source LLC
Chambersburg PA
CBHW081846280526
45789CB00007B/2583